LIFE'S TREASU

On Love

H. JACKSON BROWN, JR.

Published in Nashville, Tennessee, by Rutledge Hill
Press, a Thomas Nelson Company, P.O. Box
141000, Nashville, Tennessee 37214.

Book design by Karen Phillips and Nikita Pristouris

ISBN: 1-55853-801-1

Printed in the United States of America

1 2 3 4 5 6 7 8 9 — 04 03 02 01 00

Introduction

Imagine a world without love and romance. No love poems or love letters. No Romeo and Juliet. No Sir Lancelot and Guinevere. No Clark and Lois. No Mickey and Minnie. No heart-shaped boxes of chocolates or long-stemmed roses that say, "I'll love you forever." No heights of passion or depths of despair.

In love, we are at our best and our silliest. In love, we are the only two people on the planet, certain that no others have felt the same way we do.

Love can come at a first glance across a crowded room or it can creep up on us, growing slowly like the tendrils of a morning glory vine until it suddenly bursts into flower one sunny day.

Love has many faces. Young love is wild and outrageous, laughing at moderation and blinding us to common sense. Mature love is composed and sustaining; a celebration of commitment, companionship, and trust.

It is the lucky man and woman who experiences both.

The poet John Dryden called love "a noble madness." To Cole Porter, it was "that old black magic." The Beatles convinced us that "all you need is love." As the entries in this book reveal, love is all that and much, much more.

$\mathcal{L}$ove is when
the other person's
happiness is
more important
than your own.

Love is like
wildflowers.
It's often found
in the most
unlikely places.

Treasure the love
you receive above all.
It will survive long
after your gold
and good health
have vanished.

—OG MANDINO

$\mathcal{B}$e patient.
Be kind.
Be faithful.

Perfect love casts out fear.

—1 JOHN 4:18

*B*uy a box of children's
valentines and hide them
around the house for
your sweetheart to find
throughout the year.

Love consists in this, that two
solitudes protect and touch
and greet each other.

—RAINER MARIA RILKE

To love someone
is to see a miracle
invisible to others.

—FRANÇOIS MAURIAC

◉

At the touch of love
everyone becomes a poet.

—PLATO

$\mathcal{B}$elieve in love
at first sight.

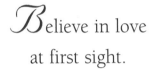

$\mathcal{N}$ever stop
the wooing.

When picking up your sweetheart at the airport, be waiting at the gate with a bouquet of balloons or flowers.

$\mathscr{I}$'ve learned that…

. . . you're never too old to be bitten by the love bug.

—AGE 81

. . . a homemade banana cream pie will impress a man more than a new dress and a new hairdo.

—AGE 44

$\mathcal{T}$ake long, hand-holding moonlit walks.

$\mathcal{D}$on't eat onions unless she does.

$\mathcal{D}$on't let her drive on slick tires.

How do I love thee?
   Let me count the ways.
I love thee to the depth and
   breadth and height my
   soul can reach. . . .
I love thee with the breath,
   smiles, tears, of all my life!
   —and, if God choose,
I shall but love thee better
   after death.

—Elizabeth Barrett Browning

*T*ell her how terrific
she's looking.

❧

*S*urprise her with a box of
Godiva chocolates.

❧

*P*ut a love note in his
shaving kit before he leaves
on a business trip.

Young Love

The hardest thing to wait for
is your first kiss.

—Age 16

The sweetest sound of all is
that of my own name spoken
by a boy I care about.

—Age 18

Don't be afraid to love.
You have the memories forever.

—Age 14

Frankie and Johnny were
    lovers, my gawd, how they
    could love,
Swore to be true to each other,
    true as the stars above;
He was her man,
    but he done her wrong.

—TRADITIONAL BALLAD

*C*ompose your own special
toast to each other.

*B*ring home her
favorite magazine.

*R*espect each other's
need for privacy.

$\mathcal{T}$o love and
be loved is the
greatest joy
in the world.

A man may be
said to love most truly
that woman in whose
company he can feel
drowsy in comfort.

—GEORGE JEAN NATHAN

I've learned that…

. . . you know you're in
love when the same person
who makes you so happy
can make you so mad.

—AGE 21

. . . you should never spend a
lot of money on the first date.

—AGE 19

And hand in hand, on
the edge of the sand,
They danced by the light
of the moon,
The moon,
The moon,
They danced by the light
of the moon.

—EDWARD LEAR

The love that we

have in our youth

is superficial

compared to the love

that an old man

has for his wife.

—WILL DURANT

I have spread my dreams
under your feet;
Tread softly because you
tread on my dreams.

—WILLIAM BUTLER YEATS

♥

Unable are the Loved to die
For Love is immortality.

—EMILY DICKINSON

Love is of all passions
the strongest, for it attacks
simultaneously the head,
the heart, and the senses.

—VOLTAIRE

A person in love mistakes
a pimple for a dimple.

It is best to love
wisely, no doubt;
but to love foolishly
is better than not to
be able to love at all.

—William Makepeace Thackeray

$\mathcal{I}$'ve learned that…

. . . the best weight-loss
program is a broken heart.

—AGE 23

. . . one of the greatest gifts
my parents gave me was
their love for each other.

—AGE 16

Shut up and kiss me.

—MARY CHAPIN CARPENTER

What appears at first sight
extremely heavy, love will
make most light.

—CHRISTOPHER HARVEY

Love is like an
hourglass, with the
heart filling up as
the brain empties.

—JULES RENARD

And then I asked him with
my eyes to ask again yes
and then he asked
me would I yes . . .
and his heart was going
like mad and yes I said
yes I will Yes.

—JAMES JOYCE

The heart that loves is
forever young.

—GREEK PROVERB

Man's love is of man's
life a thing apart;
'Tis woman's whole
existence.

—LORD BYRON

$\mathcal{T}$ake good care
of those you love.

The magic of first love
is our ignorance that
it can ever end.

—Benjamin Disraeli

*A man falls in love
through his eyes,
a woman through
her ears.*

—WOODROW WYATT

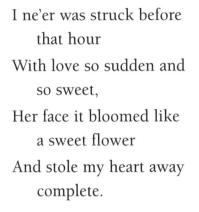

I ne'er was struck before
    that hour
With love so sudden and
    so sweet,
Her face it bloomed like
    a sweet flower
And stole my heart away
    complete.

—JOHN CLARE

It's impossible to love
and to be wise.

—Francis Bacon

Love gives us in a moment
what we can hardly attain by
effort after years of toil.

—Goethe

That Love is
all there is,
Is all we know
of Love.

—EMILY DICKINSON

$\mathscr{I}$'ve learned that…

…once a relationship is over, if you experienced more smiles than tears, then it wasn't a waste of time.

—AGE 26

…listening to sad country songs is the last thing you should do after a breakup.

—AGE 24

You are always new.
The last of your
kisses was even the
sweetest; the last
smile the brightest;
the last movement
the gracefullest.

—JOHN KEATS

Young Love

When you like a boy, all you
do is wonder if he likes you.
Then he asks you out, and all
you do is wonder if he will
break up with you.

—AGE 15

If you kiss someone on the back
of the neck, it spreads.

—AGE 16

If ever two were one,
then surely we.
If ever man were loved
by wife, then thee.

—ANNE BRADSTREET

A woman unsatisfied must
have luxuries. But a
woman who loves a man
would sleep on a board.

—D. H. LAWRENCE

The mistake we make is
when we seek to be loved,
instead of loving.
What makes us cowardly is
the fear of losing that love.

—CHARLOTTE YONGE

Love comforteth like
sunshine after rain.

—WILLIAM SHAKESPEARE

$\mathcal{I}$'ve learned that…

. . . you know you're in love when you want to tell everyone about it, even though they haven't asked.

—AGE 27

. . . just because he says he'll call you doesn't mean he will.

—AGE 20

In the degree that we love
will we be loved.

—RALPH WALDO TRINE

Love is friendship set on fire.

—JEREMY TAYLOR

An old man in love is like a
flower in winter.

—OLD PROVERB

There is nothing holier,
    in this life of ours,
than the first consciousness
    of love—
the first fluttering of its
    silken wings.

—HENRY WADSWORTH LONGFELLOW

How much better is your
love than wine.

—Song of Solomon 4:10

♥

*L*ove suddenly
makes everything
seem possible.

Slow dance.

$\mathcal{M}$ake your anniversary
an all-day event.

$\mathcal{H}$old hands in the
movies.

*Love is
the only gold.*

—ALFRED, LORD TENNYSON

If you have it, you don't
need to have anything
else, and if you don't have
it, it doesn't much matter
what else you have.

—James M. Barrie

An archeologist is
the best husband any
woman could have. The older
she gets, the more
interested he is in her.

—Agatha Christie

I'll think of another way
to get him back. After all,
tomorrow is another day.

—Scarlett O'Hara

I've learned that…

. . . I love to open my eyes when my husband is kissing me so that I can see his eyes closed while he is kissing me.

—AGE 31

. . . the older I get, the more pretty girls I remember kissing as a young man.

—AGE 84

*The way to love
anything is to realize
it might be lost.*

—G. K. CHESTERTON

And stand together yet not
  too near together:
For the pillars of the temple
  stand apart,
And the oak tree and cypress
  grow not in each other's
  shadow.

—KAHLIL GIBRAN

Drink to me only with
thine eyes,
And I will pledge with
mine;
And leave a kiss but
in the cup,
And I'll not look for wine.

—BEN JONSON

$\mathcal{T}$o explain a romantic breakup, simply say, "It was all my fault."

$\mathcal{L}$augh at her jokes.

$\mathcal{W}$atch his favorite TV program with him— even if you don't like it.

Love is like the measles;
all the worse when it comes late.

—Douglas Jerrold

'Tis better to have loved and lost
Than never to have loved at all.

—Alfred, Lord Tennyson

I've learned that...

. . . it doesn't matter how
your husband squeezes the
toothpaste; the important
thing is how he squeezes you.

—AGE 54

. . . you can't get through life
without a girlfriend.

—AGE 9

Life is slippery.
We all need
a loving hand
to hold on to.

I'll tell you something
I think you'll understand,
Then I'll say that something,
I want to hold your hand.

—JOHN LENNON AND PAUL MCCARTNEY

There is no surprise
more magical than the
surprise of being loved;
it is God's finger on
man's shoulder.

—CHARLES MORGAN

*A*fter a misunderstanding,
be the first to say, "I'm sorry."

$\mathcal{W}$hen someone tells you,
"I love you," never say,
"No you don't."

❧

$\mathcal{E}$ven when you're angry,
treat each other with respect.

Young Love

A kiss on the beach when there is a full moon is the closest thing to heaven.

—AGE 16

A girl can fall in and out of love in a hurry.

—AGE 15

Love reckons hours for
months, and days for years;
and every little
absence is an age.

—JOHN DRYDEN

Let no one who loves be
called altogether unhappy.
Even love unreturned
has its rainbow.

—JAMES M. BARRIE

$\mathcal{N}$ever give an
anniversary gift that
has to be plugged in.

❦

$\mathcal{D}$evelop a hobby you
both enjoy.

❦

$\mathcal{T}$ake dance lessons together.

$\mathcal{I}$'ve learned that...

... everything sounds
romantic in a foreign
language, no matter what
is said.

—AGE 27

... a woman never gets
too old not to want to be
held in a man's arms.

—AGE 68

$\mathcal{S}$end her flowers
where she works.

$\mathcal{S}$pend time with
other happy couples.

$\mathcal{T}$ake some silly photos of
the two of you in an
instant-photo booth.

$\mathcal{B}$uy her a cuddly
teddy bear.

The sound of a kiss is
not so loud as that of
a cannon, but its echo lasts
a great deal longer.

—Oliver Wendell Holmes

$\mathcal{L}$et your sweetheart
overhear you saying
wonderful things about her.

$\mathcal{R}$egardless of how
angry you are,
never sleep apart.

$\mathcal{P}$ray together.

*A*ssure your partner
that you're committed
to her and will always
be there when
she needs you.

What is Love?...
It is the morning and
the evening star.

—Sinclair Lewis

Two souls with but
a single thought,
Two hearts that beat
as one.

—Von Munch Bellinghausen

I love you.

And it's

getting worse.

—JOSEPH MORRIS

Call when you're going
to be late.

Memorize her favorite
love poem.

Keep your promises.

Love doesn't sit there
like a stone. It has to be
made like bread;
remade all the time,
made new.

—Ursula K. Le Guin

♥

All mankind loves a lover.

—Ralph Waldo Emerson

The realities of life bind us,
but love, great love,
introduces us to a universe
of unlimited possibilities.

♡

My life has been
awaiting you,
Your footfall was my
own heart's beat.

—PAUL CAVAFY

To love is to admire with
the heart; to admire is to
love with the mind.

—THEOPHILE GANTIER

I love you,
    not only for what you are,
But for what I am
    when I am with you.

—ROY CROFT

$\mathcal{I}$'ve learned that…

. . . love will break your heart, but it's worth it.

—AGE 26

. . . a kiss isn't a kiss without a smack.

—AGE 64

. . . when you're in love, it shows.

—AGE 28

She was a child and I was a
child,
In this kingdom by the sea,
But we loved with a love that
was more than love—
I and my Annabel Lee.

—Edgar Allan Poe

It's curious how,
when you're in love,
you yearn to go about
doing acts of kindness
to everybody.

—P. G. WODEHOUSE

The first duty of love
is to listen.

—PAUL TILLICH

We two form a multitude.

—OVID

There is a lady sweet
    and kind,
Was never a face so pleased
    my mind;
I did but see her passing by,
And yet I love her till I die.

—ANONYMOUS

Young Love

I would rather have a
best friend than a
boyfriend, except maybe
on a Friday night.

—AGE 20

My mom is always right
about my boyfriends.

—AGE 22

$\mathscr{D}$on't be critical of
each other's friends.

$\mathscr{N}$ever discuss past loves.

*R*ead *Men Are from Mars, Women Are from Venus* by John Gray (HarperCollins).

How bold one gets when one is sure of being loved!

—SIGMUND FREUD

$\mathcal{B}$uy a little heart-shaped
pillow and put it where she
can see it every night before
she goes to sleep.

$\mathcal{S}$hare a banana split.

$\mathcal{G}$ive each other big hugs
at least twice a day.

Dinah doesn't
Treat him right
But if he'd
Shave,
Dyna-mite!
Burma-Shave

—ADVERTISING ROAD SIGN

Love and a cough
cannot be hid.

—GEORGE HERBERT

A kiss is a lovely trick
designed by nature to
stop speech when words
become superfluous.

—INGRID BERGMAN

I've learned that…

. . . you know your husband
still loves you when there
are two brownies left and
he takes the smaller one.

—AGE 39

. . . after all these years, I still
have a crush on my husband.

—AGE 38

In literature as in love,
we are astonished at what
is chosen by others.

—ANDRE MAUROIS

Love is the triumph
of imagination
over intelligence.

—H. L. MENCKEN

Two such as you with such
    a master speed
Cannot be parted nor be
    swept away
From one another once you
    are agreed
That life is only life
    forevermore
Together wing to wing and
    oar to oar.

—ROBERT FROST

*P*hone your sweetheart
just to say "I love you."

*R*emind him,
"Drive safely, I love you."

*G*ive back rubs without
being asked.

Sarah, my love for
you is deathless. . . .
If I do not return,
my dear Sarah,
never forget how much
I loved you nor that when
my last breath escapes me
on the battlefield it will
whisper your name.

—Maj. Sullivan Ballou,
one week prior to his death at
the First Battle of Bull Run

$\mathcal{M}$arry only
for love.

Love like ours can
never die.

—Rudyard Kipling

Absence is to love as wind
is to fire;
It extinguishes the small
and kindles the great.

—Roger de Bussy-Rabutin

Love is what
you've been through
with somebody.

—James Thorten

Those who love deeply
never grow old;
they may die of old age,
but they die young.

—SIR ARTHUR WING PINERO

Share your dreams.

Become each other's
best friend.

♥

Forgive quickly.

Kiss slowly.

*Love conquers
all things;
let us too
surrender
to Love.*

—Virgil